JUNIOR MARTIAL ARTS
Self-Esteem

Junior Martial Arts

ALL AROUND GOOD HABITS
CONFIDENCE
CONCENTRATION
HAND-EYE COORDINATION
HANDLING PEER PRESSURE
SAFETY
SELF-DEFENSE
SELF-DISCIPLINE
SELF-ESTEEM

Junior Martial Arts
Self-Esteem

Sara James

Mason Crest

Mason Crest
450 Parkway Drive, Suite D
Broomall, PA 19008
www.masoncrest.com

Printed and bound in the United States of America.

First printing
9 8 7 6 5 4 3 2 1

Series ISBN: 978-1-4222-2731-2
ISBN: 978-1-4222-2740-4
ebook ISBN: 978-1-4222-9073-6

The Library of Congress has cataloged the
hardcopy format(s) as follows:

Library of Congress Cataloging-in-Publication Data

James, Sara.
  Self-esteem / Sara James.
     pages cm. – (Junior martial arts)
     ISBN 978-1-4222-2740-4 (hardcover) – ISBN 978-1-4222-2731-2 (series) –
ISBN 978-1-4222-9073-6 (ebook)
  1. Martial arts–Juvenile literature. 2. Self-esteem–Juvenile literature. I. Title.
  GV1101.35.J368 2014
  796.8–dc23
                                        2013004762

Publisher's notes:
The websites mentioned in this book were active at the time of publication. The publisher is not responsible for websites that have changed their addresses or discontinued operation since the date of publication. The publisher will review and update the website addresses each time the book is reprinted.

Contents

MORE THAN FIGHTING

Chances are, you've seen some martial arts. Maybe you've seen an actor doing martial arts in a movie. Or your friends take martial arts classes. Maybe you just started practicing martial arts yourself.

Most people think martial arts are all about fighting. They think martial arts are about kicking and punching. Some people think martial arts are about beating up someone who's attacking you.

If you know anything about martial arts, you know that's not true. Sure, you do learn some kicks and punches. But you know that martial arts students never use what they learn unless they have to. Martial arts aren't about hurting others.

You only use martial arts for self-defense. If someone is attacking you, you can use martial arts to get away.

You should never use martial arts to hurt people. You don't use them in school to hurt or pick on other kids. You don't use them on your brothers and sisters at home.

There's a lot more to martial arts than just fighting. You learn the moves. But you also learn all sorts of other things in martial arts class.

Understanding Martial Arts

All martial arts are ways of **defending** yourself. There are different kinds of martial arts. They're all a little bit different from each other.

Some martial arts are more famous than others. You might already have heard about karate, for example. Karate comes from Japan. It means "empty hand." That's because people who practice karate don't usually use weapons. Instead, karate has a lot of punches, arm blocks, and kicks.

Taekwondo is another popular martial art. People from all over the world practice it. It comes from Korea. Taekwondo means "way of foot and fist." There's a lot of kicking in taekwondo.

Brazilian Jiu-Jitsu

Martial arts have roots that come from lots of different places. For example, Brazilian jiu-jitsu was invented in Brazil. But it's based on jiu-jitsu and judo, which come from Japan. A jiu-jitsu teacher traveled from Japan to Brazil. He taught jiu-jitsu in his new country. People in Brazil changed it a little bit and taught it in new ways. Now, you can learn the Japanese kind or the Brazilian kind!

Some martial arts come from South America. Capoeira comes from Brazil. It's a kind of martial art that's almost like dancing or a game. Two people practice capoeira together. Other people sing while they fight.

Martial arts are usually taught in schools. A school is called a dojo. Dojos have teachers. Martial arts students might call their teacher "sensei." Sensei is a Japanese word for teacher. Students might also call the teacher "master."

People who want to learn martial arts have a lot of choices. There are schools for every kind of martial art all over the world. And there are hundreds of kinds of martial arts!

If you want to take martial arts, look around for the right school. There might be a few to choose from. You can try out different kinds. You'll find a school with the right martial art and the right teacher.

Being a Better Person

Learning the moves of karate or capoeira is just one part of martial arts. It's the easiest part to see. When you go see a martial arts movie, you only see the fancy jumps and flying kicks on screen. You don't see the other things the actor had to learn to become a martial arts master.

Martial arts can help you be a better person. There are lots of ways martial arts can help you out!

Martial arts can help you do better at school. Maybe school is hard for you. You might have trouble paying attention in class or finishing your homework. You might not get the grades you want.

Taking martial arts classes can help with your school trouble. In martial arts class, you can learn all sorts of new things. You learn how to concentrate. That means you learn how to pay attention to your sensei. You also pay attention to what your body is doing. In order to get better at a martial art, you have to think really hard while you practice.

You can use what you learn in martial arts at school. Before, you might have had a hard time paying attention to the teacher in class. Maybe you never could sit still long enough to read books. Maybe you didn't finish your homework.

But martial arts can teach you how to concentrate. Now you can sit still and listen to your teacher more often. You finish books and homework. You're learning more. And you end up getting better grades!

Martial arts can also help you be a better friend. Maybe you get in fights a lot with your friends. Maybe you have a hard time getting along with others.

Martial arts can teach you how to respect others. When you respect others, you think about their feelings. You are nice to them.

In martial arts class, you learn how to respect people. You learn how to respect the teacher. That means you listen to her. You follow her directions. You don't talk while she's talking to the class.

You learn to respect your martial arts classmates too. You don't tell them they're bad at a move. You don't push them out of the way. You learn how to tell people they're doing things well.

Learning to respect others will make you a better friend. You start thinking about your friends' feelings. You don't shout at them. You don't push them around. You're a lot nicer to them.

Martial arts aren't magic. They can't make your life perfect. But martial arts can teach you things you can use all the time. Martial arts are about making your body strong. But they can also change the way you think about yourself and others.

Self-Esteem

Martial arts can teach you about self-esteem. Self-esteem is how good you feel about who you are and what you can do.

We can have high self-esteem. If you have high self-esteem, you like yourself a lot. You think you should have good friends and a family. You feel good about yourself. You're proud about what you can do and try hard to get better at the things you aren't that good at.

If you have low self-esteem, you don't like yourself very much. You might not think you're very smart. You might not think you should be happy. Maybe you don't think you're good at anything.

It's much better to have high self-esteem. Having lots of self-esteem doesn't mean you think you're better than other people. It just means you like yourself. High self-esteem changes the way you see yourself. When you respect yourself, you make better choices. You do what's really best for you.

Where does self-esteem come from? It comes from inside of you. It also comes from other people.

If you always tell yourself that you're doing your best and that you're a good person, you'll have high self-esteem. You'll feel good about yourself. If you always tell yourself you're no good, you might end up with low self-esteem. You won't feel good about who you are.

Other people also give us low or high self-esteem. If people always tell you you're bad at something, you might start to believe them. If everyone around you points out all the things you do wrong, pretty soon you may have low self-esteem. The things people are saying might not be true. But you'll still feel bad.

But if everyone you know tells you good things about yourself, the opposite happens. People tell you you've done a good job. Or that you're a good person. Then you'll have high self-esteem.

We all have trouble with self-esteem sometimes. It's okay to feel bad about yourself sometimes. But the best way to live is to like yourself. You'll be much happier with high self-esteem!

Martial arts can help you get more self-esteem. Learning martial arts can teach you to like yourself more. You'll be excited about all the new things you can do. You'll feel good about yourself in martial arts class. Over time, you'll feel good about yourself outside of martial arts class too.

Self-Esteem and Confidence

Have you ever heard of self-confidence? It's kind of like self-esteem. But it's a little different. When you're confident, you know you can do something. You can be confident that you'll be able to learn that next judo move. Or you can be confident that you'll get an A in math. Self-esteem is a bigger idea. It's about how you feel about yourself and how much you like yourself. You could be confident that you'll get an A, but still not like yourself very much. It's good to have both confidence and self-esteem.

SELF-ESTEEM AND MARTIAL ARTS

Taking a martial arts class is one way to get more self-esteem. You won't have more self-esteem overnight, though. You have to work hard at it. Pretty soon, you'll see you like yourself a lot more!

"Good Job"

When you take martial arts, you'll hear a lot of **encouragement**. Every day, someone will probably tell you something good. After you do a tricky move, the teacher might say, "Great job," or, "I knew you could do it."

You'll get thanked for your hard work. Everyone will be saying nice things to you. You'll start saying them to other people too.

Self-esteem is about how you see yourself and how you feel about who you are. You can't always feel great, but building your self-esteem through martial arts is a good way to start to feel better.

Even if you can't do something yet, no one will tell you can't do it. When you're practicing a new kick, people will tell you to keep trying. Your teacher might give you some advice. But he won't tell you you're stupid or bad at martial arts.

You'll get used to hearing good things. When you get a lot of encouragement, you start to feel good about yourself and what you can do.

Imagine if everyone in class only told you how bad you were. You would feel pretty terrible. You'd think you couldn't do anything.

Instead, you feel the opposite. You feel like you can do lots of things! And that's part of having self-esteem.

New Moves

Everyone has to do sports sometime or another. It could be in gym class. Or playing after school. Or on a sports team.

Some people want to play a lot of sports. And some people are really good at them. But not everyone can be good at sports without practicing.

Sometimes that makes people feel bad. Getting picked last for a team isn't a good feeling. Neither is getting teased for not playing well.

Martial arts can help you get better at sports. When you practice martial arts, you're really practicing all sorts of things. You're practicing being flexible, so you can move around in new ways. You're practicing hand-eye coordination. That's how well your eyes and hands work together.

Flexibility and hand-eye coordination help you outside of martial arts. For example, you can throw and catch balls better with good hand-eye coordination. That helps you out in all kinds of sports.

Even if you don't get a lot better at sports, you'll still feel good about yourself. You'll know you can do martial arts moves.

And you won't feel like a bad person if you're not a sports star. Because you have self-esteem and like yourself, you can stop worrying about not being great at sports.

Level Up

Making goals is a big part of martial arts. Goals are things you want to do. Your goal might be to learn a new taekwondo kick. You might make getting a good grade on your next test your goal.

Setting goals for yourself can really help your self-esteem. When you set out to do something and do it, you feel good about yourself.

In martial arts, you can make small goals or big goals. A small goal would be to learn one new move in martial arts class. Maybe you want to practice at home once a week.

A bigger goal would be getting to the highest level in your martial art. Or to some day become a teacher.

It's better to start out with small goals. It's easier to work toward them. Let's say you want to learn your first kick.

You watch your teacher when she shows you how to do it. Then you practice. You listen when she gives you tips on how to do it. You practice again.

You keep practicing for the next two classes. Your teacher comes over again, and tells you that you've got it!

How do you think you'd feel? You'd probably be pretty happy! With some practice, you reached your goal. So you feel good about yourself.

Now think about if this happened all the time. You could make new goals every week. Pretty soon, you'll feel really good about what you can do. You'll like yourself more because you succeeded.

You can also work toward big goals. Maybe you want to be a black belt in your karate school. Becoming a black belt will take a long time. You have to work for years to get a black belt.

Reaching for a goal like getting a new belt can help you to feel better about yourself. Meeting goals can make you see that you can do whatever you set your mind to.

Belt Colors

A lot of martial arts use belts colors. Each belt color is a different level. In jiu-jitsu, a new student starts out with a white belt. Then he gets a yellow belt. Then blue, green, purple, and brown. After he gets really good, he gets a black belt. But it doesn't end there. There are ten levels of black belt. A martial artist is always learning! Your jiu-jitsu school might use different colors at different levels. But the idea is the same. Every time you learn a new set of things, you move up to the next level.

But picture getting your black belt. You would feel really great! You would be proud of how much work you put into it. Each goal you reached along the way gave you some more self-esteem. And getting your black belt gives you a lot of self-esteem!

Getting Better at Martial Arts

As you go to more martial arts classes, your self-esteem gets better. And the better your self-esteem is, the better you are at martial arts!

Think of it this way. At first, you might not really feel great about who you are. Maybe you think you're really bad at martial arts. You don't think you'll get any better.

Maybe you don't try very hard because of your low self-esteem. You don't want other people in class to see how bad you are. So you hide in a corner. You only try new moves once or twice and then give up.

But you get better every time you go to class. Your teacher tells you you're doing great. You learn new moves. You move up a level and get a new belt.

You feel a lot better about yourself after reaching a goal. You don't think you're bad anymore. And best of all, you like yourself more!

You also get better at martial arts. Instead of hiding in the corner, you practice in the middle of the room. You try moves over and over again and you get them right really fast. Because you have more self-esteem, you can do better with martial arts.

IMPROVING YOUR SELF-ESTEEM

3

Having high self-esteem is a good thing. It's great to like yourself and feel good about who you are.

Lots of people have low self-esteem, though. They don't feel very good about themselves. We all have to go through that once in a while. Everyone feels bad sometimes.

But if you don't have much self-esteem, don't worry. You can always change that! Luckily, there are lots of ways to build self-esteem.

Think Good Thoughts

The best thing you can do to keep your self-esteem high is to think good things about yourself. Let's say you're sitting down to work on homework. You could think, "I'm so bad at school." "I can't do this." "I'm going to get a bad grade." Those thoughts will make you feel bad.

Instead, think, "I can do this." Think, "I'm going to do well on this homework."

These kinds of **positive** thoughts will make you feel good. And when you feel good, you can probably do better on your homework. And when you get a good grade, your self-esteem goes up!

How can you practice thinking good things about yourself? How can you hold on to positive thoughts? You can do lots of things to learn how to like yourself. List everything you're good at. Think hard and be honest. Do you play an instrument? Do you draw well? Are you good at science? If you can't think of things, ask other people. Your family should be able to add lots of things to your list. Ask your friends for more!

You could build your self-esteem by giving yourself three compliments every day. That means you should tell yourself three nice things. You usually compliment other people. You might tell your parents that they cooked a really good dinner. You might tell your best friend that she made a really nice drawing. To build your self-esteem, tell yourself those things instead! If you made a goal in soccer, tell yourself, "Great job!" Or give yourself a compliment for helping your dad do the dishes.

After a while, thinking positive thoughts will be normal. You won't want to think bad things about yourself. You'll learn to like yourself more!

Find Good Friends

Part of self-esteem is what other people think about you. If everyone around you says mean things about you, you might have low self-esteem.

It's important to find people who are nice to you. You want friends who don't tell you you're bad at sports or stupid.

If you have friends who are mean to you, think about finding some new friends. Are there people who seem nice at school? What about on your sports team? Or in your afterschool class?

Try getting to know some new people. Make sure they say nice things to you and to other people. And be sure to be nice to them too! The best friendships are about being kind to each other.

Practicing martial arts can be a great way to build your self-esteem. Martial arts are about training your body, but they're also about changing the way you think. You can learn respect for others, good listening, and feel better about yourself.

Mistakes

Everyone makes mistakes. You might make a mistake on a test. Or forget what time swim practice is and miss it. You may play a wrong note in a band practice.

You can't be perfect all the time. It's not fair to think you can be. No one is! So don't be hard on yourself when you make a mistake.

Every time you make a mistake, you can learn from it. You can figure out how to make sure you don't make the same mistake again. When you get your test back with the right answer written in, you learn. After you forget swim practice once, you write it down so you remember the next one. You practice your instrument and play the right note in the next concert.

Talk to Someone

It's hard to deal with low self-esteem. Sometimes it's really hard. Maybe something happened that makes you feel really bad about yourself.

Talking with another person about how you're feeling can be a good way to deal with negative feelings. At school, guidance counselors can help you work through bad feelings and help you feel better.

Maybe you move to a new town. You feel bad because you haven't made any friends yet. Maybe someone is teasing you at school. Whatever the problem is, it makes you not like yourself very much.

You can always go talk to someone if you feel really bad. You could talk to a friend you're really close to. A good friend will listen. They won't make fun of you.

Or you could talk to an adult. You could talk to your mom or dad or other family member.

At school, you can always talk to your guidance counselor. Guidance counselors are there to talk to kids about their problems. You can trust guidance counselors. They can help you deal with things like low self-esteem.

Martial Arts Practice

You can also practice self-esteem in martial arts. And you can use what you learn in martial arts class in other parts of your life. The skills you learn in martial arts can help you in school, with friends, and with your family.

Listen to your martial arts teacher! He'll give you lots of encouragement. He'll help you get better at the things you haven't quite figured out yet.

Don't get mad if your teacher gives you help. She isn't doing it because you're bad. She just wants to make sure you get the move right. If you aren't okay with getting help, you won't get better at martial arts.

Pay attention to what you're thinking in class too. Are you thinking, "I'll never get this move right"? Or "I'm so bad at martial arts"? That won't get you anywhere!

Turn those thoughts around. Think good things instead. Think, "I can get this move if I practice some more." Think, "I've already gotten a lot better at martial arts."

You'll feel good about yourself and what you're doing. And you'll be a better martial artist.

SELF-ESTEEM AND YOUR LIFE

Having high self-esteem is very important. It makes your life a lot better. It doesn't just make martial arts class better. But it also makes school, getting along with friends, and spending time with your family better too!

School

Self-esteem has a lot to do with school. It can be easy to put yourself down all the time at school. You might feel stupid if you don't get an A on a test. Or feel bad because you don't do well at gym or art or music.

But when you have high self-esteem, school is a lot easier! You don't get upset every time you don't do something perfectly. You know you're a good person. It doesn't matter if you don't get perfect grades. Or if you're not great at dodge ball or painting.

No one likes being teased or bullied. But with high self-esteem, you won't let what others think or say hurt your feelings. You'll feel better about yourself and others will be able to see your confidence.

ADHD, Self-Esteem, and Taekwondo

Lots of kids have attention-deficit hyperactivity disorder (ADHD). They have a lot of energy or find paying attention really hard. Kids with ADHD sometimes have low self-esteem because it's hard to make friends or to do well at school. Luckily, taekwondo can help. Abbey is a girl with ADHD. She was having a hard time fitting in and felt bad about herself. Then she started taking taekwondo lessons. How did it help? On ADDitude, a website about ADHD, her mom describes a test where Abbey had to break a board in half. She was afraid Abbey couldn't do it. But "Abbey said, 'Cool,' kicked the board in two, and flashed me a grin." She had enough self-esteem to believe she could break a wooden board!

High self-esteem might even help you do better in school. Imagine you have to write a book report. Then you have to stand up in front of the class and tell everyone about the book you read.

For a lot of people, that sounds scary! If you have low self-esteem, you think, "I'm not going to be able to talk in front of everyone. I won't write a good book report. And no one will listen to me talk." If you tell yourself these things, you might not do very well. You might not try very hard on your book report. In front of the class, you might speak quietly, or talk really, really fast.

If you have high self-esteem, the book report is a lot easier. You'd say to yourself, "I'm nervous, but I can do it. I love books, so writing a book report isn't so bad. I'll be okay." You try hard to write a good report. And even though you're nervous, you'd do your best talking in front of the class.

High self-esteem can help you get better grades and like school more. When you have high self-esteem, you try hard because you know you can do well.

Other Kids

With more self-esteem, your friendships will get better. When you don't have much self-esteem, you might not like to try new things. You may think you'll be bad at something new. So if your friends invite you to try bowling with them, or take a martial arts class, you might say no. But your friends want you to say yes!

You can have a lot more fun with your friends if you're not worrying about yourself. If you always think you're no good, you won't have much fun with your friends. And your friends want you to feel good about yourself!

If you have high self-esteem, you can also deal with bullies. Bullies are people who are mean to others. They call people names, and sometimes even hurt other people.

Bullies often have low self-esteem. They might make fun of others because they feel bad about themselves. They may want to make other people feel sad or angry like they do.

If you have high self-esteem, you can fight bullies. But not with martial arts moves! You can fight back by not caring what they say. If you like yourself a lot, then it doesn't matter what a bully says about you. You don't have to listen to

them. Martial arts aren't about hurting bullies or others. They're about having the self-esteem you need to not care about what mean people think.

Self-esteem is a great thing to have. You have to work hard for high self-esteem. But it's worth it! And martial arts are a great way to get self-esteem. No matter what martial art you choose, you're sure to feel proud about yourself in no time. And that means you'll like yourself more!

Words to Know:

concentrate: To focus on one thing.

defending: Stopping another person from hurting you.

encouragement: Positive words that push you to do your best and stick with an activity.

flexible: Able to bend or stretch the body.

positive: Something that makes you feel good.

respect: Treating others the way you want to be treated. This can mean listening to your teachers and friends or thinking of others' feelings.

Find Out More

Online

Kidshealth: Self-Esteem
kidshealth.org/teen/your_mind/emotions/self_esteem.html

Martial Arts Museum
martialartsmuseum.com

Women and Children's Health Network
www.cyh.com/HealthTopics/HealthTopicDetailsKids.aspx?p=335&np=
    287&id=1588

In Books

Goggerly, Liz. *Capoeira: Fusing Dance and Martial Arts*. Minneapolis, Minn.: Lerner
    Publishing Group, 2011.

Moss, Wendy L. *Being Me: A Kid's Guide to Boosting Confidence and Self-Esteem*.
    Washington, D.C.: Magination Press, 2010.

Wiseman, Blaine. *Martial Arts*. New York: AV2 Books, 2010.

Index

About the Author

Sara James is a writer and blogger. She writes educational books for children on a variety of topics, including health, history, and current events.

Picture Credits

www.Dreamstime.com
   Andreblais: p. 24
   Forsterforest: p. 14
   Joeygil: p. 12
   Judwick: p. 18
   Lisafx: p. 22
   Monkeybusinessimages: p. 26
   Shaunwilkinson: p. 16
   Tvphotos: p. 6
   Vhamrick: p. 21